YOU

GOT

THIS

YOU GOT THIS

Compiled by Peggy Jones

An Hachette UK Company
www.hachette.co.uk

Summersdale Publishers Ltd
Part of Octopus Publishing Group Limited
Carmelite House
50 Victoria Embankment
LONDON
EC4Y 0DZ
UK

www.summersdale.com

Printed and bound in China

ISBN: 978-1-80007-391-3

Substantial discounts on bulk quantities of Summersdale books are available to corporations, professional associations and other organizations. For details contact general enquiries: telephone: +44 (0) 1243 771107 or email: enquiries@summersdale.com.

To......................................

From..................................

Believe in your heart what you know to be true about yourself.

Mary J. Blige

Realness
over
perfection

You are
beautiful
and you can
do anything.

Lizzo

HOPE IS THE MOST EXCITING THING THERE IS IN LIFE.

Mandy Moore

PICK
YOURSELF
BACK UP
AND TRY
AGAIN

The great secret of getting what you want from life is to know what you want and believe you can have it.

Norman Vincent Peale

It's so much harder to not be yourself than to just be yourself.

Tatyana Ali

This is a new story you're writing

Live in the moment. Enjoy the day. Make the most of what you have.

Michael J. Fox

I really don't think
life is about the
I-could-have-beens.
Life is only about
the I-tried-to-do.

Nikki Giovanni

Try YOUR best – not someone else's

Energy and persistence conquer all things.

Benjamin Franklin

Some people
say you are
going the wrong
way when it's
simply a way
of your own.

Angelina Jolie

YOUR INTUITION IS YOUR POWER

If you lie to anybody on the planet, don't lie to that person reflected in the mirror.

Betty White

There is no way to be perfect and no fun in being perfect.

Alicia Keys

YOU
CONTAIN
ENDLESS
POSSIBILITIES

There is
nothing either
good or bad,
but thinking
makes it so.

William Shakespeare

A champion is defined not by their wins but by how they can recover when they fall.

Serena Williams

You owe yourself kindness

Fear kills your ability to see beauty. You have to get beyond fear.

Will Smith

JUST PLAY.
HAVE FUN.
ENJOY THE GAME.

Michael Jordan

BE THE
REASON
YOU SMILE
TODAY

I avoid
looking forward
or backward,
and try to
keep looking
upward.

Charlotte Brontë

Don't give up trying to do what you really want to do.

Ella Fitzgerald

Sometimes
Plan B
is meant
to be

Your life is already a miracle of chance waiting for you to shape its destiny.

Toni Morrison

You've got to value yourself and know that you're worth everything.

Jennifer Lopez

Make your stumble part of the dance

There are talkers enough among us; I'll be one of the doers.

Charles Dickens

Courage is
resistance to
fear, mastery
of fear – not
absence of fear.

Mark Twain

IF YESTERDAY IS HEAVY, PUT IT DOWN

You've got to get out there and make it happen for yourself.

Diana Ross

You must do the thing you think you cannot do.

Eleanor Roosevelt

THERE'S
NO RUSH IF
YOU'RE STILL
PLANNING
YOUR ROUTE

The most
important
relationship
is the one
you have with
yourself.

Diane von Fürstenberg

We must
accept finite
disappointment,
but never lose
infinite hope.

Martin Luther King Jr

Enjoy the beauty of becoming

Opportunities
multiply as they
are seized.

Sun Tzu

ONLY DO WHAT YOUR HEART TELLS YOU.

Diana, Princess of Wales

YOU
DESERVE
KINDNESS

Be gentle with yourself and remember there's no one way up that mountain.

Jonathan Van Ness

Act as if what you do makes a difference. It does.

William James

You are
the hero of
your story

Nothing can dim the light which shines from within.

Maya Angelou

I am the
greatest.
I said that
even before
I knew I was.

Muhammad Ali

Never put a price on your peace

You'd be surprised – you are much stronger than you think.

Lady Gaga

If something
stands between
you and your
success - move it.
Never be denied.

Dwayne Johnson

**YOU CAN
MAKE IT
THROUGH
TODAY**

Never bend your head. Always hold it high. Look the world straight in the eye.

Helen Keller

Life is like riding a bicycle. To keep your balance, you must keep moving.

Albert Einstein

ONE DAY, ALL THIS WILL MAKE SENSE

Take a step back,
stay strong,
stay grounded
and press on.

LL Cool J

The most effective way to do it is to do it.

Amelia Earhart

Start by believing in yourself

I am
deliberate
and afraid
of nothing.

Audre Lorde

IT'S ALL ABOUT WHAT MAKES YOU FEEL GOOD.

Billie Eilish

GIVE UNDER-THINKING A TRY

It's never too late
– never too late
to start over,
never too late to
be happy.

Jane Fonda

You have power over your mind – not outside events. Realize this, and you will find strength.

Marcus Aurelius

Don't ignore your dreams –
you dreamed them for a reason

You are enough just as you are.

Meghan,
Duchess of Sussex

Life is very
interesting…
in the end, some
of your greatest
pains become your
greatest strengths.

Drew Barrymore

You
deserve
good
things

Am I good enough? Yes, I am.

Michelle Obama

I have always been
delighted at the
prospect of a new
day… with perhaps a
bit of magic waiting
somewhere behind
the morning.

J. B. Priestley

BELIEVE IT
AND YOU'LL
BECOME IT

Do what you were born to do. You have to trust yourself.

Beyoncé

You must never be fearful about what you are doing when it is right.

Rosa Parks

NEVER

GIVE UP

Let us make
our future now,
and let us make
our dreams
tomorrow's reality.

Malala Yousafzai

Life is not a problem to be solved, but a reality to be experienced.

Søren Kierkegaard

Take
a deep
breath

Being disappointed
is one thing and
being discouraged
is something else.
I am disappointed
but I am not
discouraged.

Tennessee Williams

KNOW
YOUR
WORTH.

Taraji P. Henson

TAKE A CHANCE ON YOURSELF

It's about putting one step in front of another, about forward movement to where you wanna be.

Ava DuVernay

To love oneself is the beginning of a lifelong romance.

Oscar Wilde

Show the world just what you're made of

There are
no mistakes.
Only opportunities.

Tina Fey

If you ask me
what I came into
this life to do,
I will tell you:
I came to live
out loud.

Émile Zola

Do it for the thrill

It's important not to limit yourself. You can do whatever you really love to do, no matter what it is.

Ryan Gosling

A hero is an
ordinary individual
who finds strength
to persevere and
endure in spite
of overwhelming
obstacles.

Christopher Reeve

YOUR
FUTURE IS
READY AND
WAITING
FOR YOU

Step into who you are.

Janet Mock

The secret to doing anything is believing that you can do it.

Bob Ross

YOU ARE
INCOMPARABLE

Failure is the
condiment that
gives success
its flavour.

Truman Capote

Just forget
about it and
get up and
do it again.

JoJo Siwa

Self-love runs deepest of all

You are on
the eve of a
complete victory.
You can't go wrong.
The world is
behind you.

Josephine Baker

I AM MADE AND REMADE CONTINUALLY.

Virginia Woolf

YOU'RE
GOING TO
MAKE IT

However difficult life may seem, there's always something you can do and succeed at.

Stephen Hawking

Nothing is impossible. The word itself says, "I'm possible!"

Audrey Hepburn

Your own
light is
showing
you the
way

**Our action
creates our
destiny. Our joy
creates space
for our freedom.**

Tracee Ellis Ross

Not everything
that is faced can
be changed; but
nothing can be
changed until
it is faced.

James Baldwin

Keep
pushing
through

Make way for the unprecedented and watch your reality rearrange yourself.

Yrsa Daley-Ward

What lies behind
you and what lies
in front of you
pales in comparison
to what lies
inside you.

Ralph Waldo Emerson

**TAKE
WHAT YOU
DESERVE**

You learn a lot from your mistakes. You have to take risks and make mistakes.

Cate Blanchett

When you want something, all the universe conspires in helping you to achieve it.

Paulo Coelho

FEAR IS JUST A STORY WE TELL OURSELVES

Never give up.
Today is hard,
tomorrow will be
worse, but the
day after tomorrow
will be sunshine.

Jack Ma

We can only see
a short distance
ahead, but we
can see plenty
there that needs
to be done.

Alan Turing

Difficult doesn't mean impossible

I don't know
what my path
is yet. I'm just
walking on it.

Olivia Newton-John

MARCH
TO YOUR
OWN BEAT.

Zoë Kravitz

EVEN SMALL
WINS CAN
ADD UP
TO BIG
SUCCESSES

I just have to be myself. I'm not perfect and I'm going to make mistakes.

Laverne Cox

It's important for you to voice out your truth.

John Boyega

Restart as
many times
as you
need to –
just don't quit

Hope is being able to see that there is light despite all of the darkness.

Harvey Milk

Courage starts
with showing
up and letting
ourselves
be seen.

Brené Brown

Show up
for yourself

One small crack does not mean that you are broken; it means that you were put to the test and you didn't fall apart.

Linda Poindexter

At the end
of the day,
we can endure
much more than
we think we can.

Frida Kahlo

IF YOU CAN'T FIND YOURSELF, CREATE YOURSELF

**The more
I hold myself
close and fully
embrace who
I am, the more
I thrive.**

Elliot Page

The struggle you're in today is developing the strength you need for tomorrow. Don't give up.

Robert Tew

YES
YOU
CAN

If you're
walking down
the right path
and you're willing
to keep walking,
eventually you'll
make progress.

Barack Obama

If you hear a voice within you say, "you cannot paint," then by all means paint, and that voice will be silenced.

Vincent van Gogh

You have more strength than you'll ever know

As soon as you trust yourself, you will know how to live.

Johann Wolfgang von Goethe

THE
MAGIC IS
INSIDE
YOU.

Dolly Parton

FIND YOUR
VERSION OF
HAPPINESS

I've finally stopped running away from myself. Who else is there better to be?

Goldie Hawn

The thing you fear most has no power. Your fear of it is what has the power.

Oprah Winfrey

Your productivity does not equal your worth

I know my own heart.

Anne Lister

Success is inner
peace. That's a
good day for me.

Denzel Washington

Don't give up now

The moment you doubt whether you can fly, you cease forever to be able to do it.

J. M. Barrie

You don't have
to be perfect
to achieve
your dreams.

Katy Perry

TURN
A WISH
INTO
WORK

You are more precious to this world than you'll ever know.

Lili Reinhart

Be bold.
Be brave
enough to
be your
true self.

Queen Latifah

TODAY,
CHOOSE
JOY

Success comes
from knowing
that you did your
best to become
the best that you
are capable of
becoming.

John Wooden

**Absorb what
is useful,
discard what
is useless
and add what
is specifically
your own.**

Bruce Lee

Moving on
is moving up

Life is long and there are plenty of opportunities to make mistakes. The point of it all is to learn.

Ethan Hawke

IT IS NOT THE MOUNTAIN WE CONQUER, BUT OURSELVES.

Edmund Hillary

IF FEAR IS YOUR REACTION, MAKE COURAGE YOUR DECISION

Never, ever be afraid to make some noise and get in good trouble, necessary trouble.

John Lewis

When I started counting my blessings, my whole life turned around.

Willie Nelson

Own
your life

Let go of the things that make you feel dead! Life is worth living!

Rihanna

Without a humble
but reasonable
confidence in
your own powers
you cannot be
successful
or happy.

Norman Vincent Peale

I'm really fine with the peaks and valleys. It's the valleys that make me, force me to reach further.

Cher

YOU

GOT

THIS

Have you enjoyed this book?
If so, find us on Facebook at
Summersdale Publishers, on Twitter
at @Summersdale and on Instagram
at @summersdalebooks and get in
touch. We'd love to hear from you!

www.summersdale.com